PEARL WHITE

WRITTEN AND ILLUSTRATED BY

RENE WHITE

I'd like to introduce
Pearl White.

She is white
and light
and bright ,
and yes, you may pat her,
she won't bite.

No, she is not a **bullDOG,**

sHe is not a **pitbull,**

She is a pure
boxer DOG,
please ignore
the DrOOL.

She is white like

vanilla ice-cream,

she is white like

untouched snow.

She is white like
cream and milk,
She is white like
the North Pole.

She is not a dog to everyone's taste

not everyone would approve,

of her ears

of her tail

of her colour,

BOXER

BOXER

LIFE IS BETTER
WITH A BOXER

but to me, she is more

than all white,

she is all

I ever desired.

Sometimes she howls
at the moon,
and once in a while
she barks
up the wrong tree,
but she is happy
with who she is,

she is herself,
and she is free.

11

She didn't pick the colour of her fur,

As far as I can recall.

She wears it well, just the same,

And she is having a ball.

She is white like
a white lion cub,
she is white like
a Beluga whale,

She is white like

a froth in a cup,

She is white like

snow in a gale.

If one day
you happen to see
something blending
with the snow,
something bouncing
like a ball,
something putting on
a show,
without a doubt, you should know,

If it barks at lemons,

if it stomps at the sight of brooms and mops,

if it tries to bite hornets and bees,

if it eats raw beans,

if it doesn't even say, "No" to tangerines,

if it's really silly,

really soft and squishy,

if it's really bright,

you just saw white boxer DOG,

better HOLD on tiGHt.

And please remember this
So that you can spot them,

They are white like
the Antarctic,
They are white like
an angry blizzard,

They are white like
Himalaya's peak,
They are white like
a beard on a wizard.

They are Pearl White.

@BoxerPearlWhite

To Pearl White and my loving boys.
To all the dogs in the world regardless of their breed or color.

Pearl's Friends

 Mr Butters
 Zeus
 Lily
 Piper

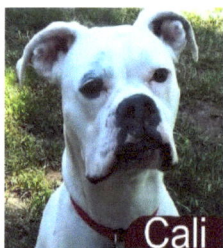 Cali
 Luna
 Stanley
 Rupert

 Mizu
 Snoopy
 Morty
 Joe

 Nahla Mae
 Teddy
 Roxanne
 Kimber

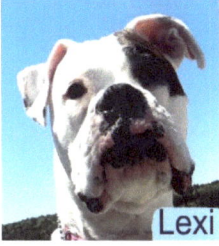 Lexi
 Albert
 Bruno
 Cosmo and Jax

 May
 Darla
 Jane
 Rallo and Roo

 Twister
 Maggie
 Asher
 Pearl

 Marvin
 Nash
 Winston & Luna
 Bruno